Hanging Out the Wash

Hanging Out the Wash

and Other Ways to Find More in Less

Adair Lara

CONARI PRESS Berkeley, California

Conari Press books are distributed by Publishers Group West.

Cover Photography: © Masayoshi Hichiwa / Photonica
Cover Design: Suzanne Albertson
Book Design: Courtnay Perry

ISBN: 1-57324-772-3

This has been previously cataloged by the
Library of Congress under this title

Lara, Adair
Slowing down in a speeded-up world/Adair Lara
p.   cm.
ISBN 0-943233-57-7 (pbk.)
1. Conduct of life. I. title.
158'.1—dc20   93-38701
                                                                CIP

Printed in the United States of America.
02 03 04 05 Data 10 9 8 7 6 5 4 3 2 1

For my mother

hanging out the wash

Coming Home to Ourselves   1

By Hand   11

Seeing Deeply   57

Taking Time   101

Acknowledgments   149

About the Author   151

Coming Home to Ourselves

When you are immersed in doing without being centered, it feels like being away from home. And when you reconnect with being, even for a few minutes, you know it immediately. You feel you are at home no matter where you are and what problems you face.

—*Jon Kabat-Zinn*

my mother must have been busy—she had seven kids—but in my memory she's always still, poised over a pot of steaming oatmeal, or holding her face up to the warm sun. She was an indifferent housekeeper and an absentminded cook, and she carried calm with her wherever she went. She used to wash our clothes in a wringer washer and then hang them on the clotheslines outside. As she pinned up each garment, she said, she thought about the child it belonged to. She never wanted a dryer, even after we could afford one, because it would steal this from her, this quiet contemplation.

I am just as busy, or busier, than my mother was, with the job and kids and my projects. But it's a different kind of busyness, a faster, jerkier one, getting one task over with and then on to the next. Thirty years after I watched my mother hang out the wash, I carry the laundry to the basement and toss in the clothes, switching them in a wet clump from washer to dryer. I am doing what she did—drying the family clothes—but not getting as much satisfaction from it.

I know I'm supposed to quit charging around and stop and smell the roses. But I get caught up, like a swimmer in a pool full of floating junk, in what's coming at me. I call the dentist for an appointment, go to lunch, meet deadlines, throw a load in the washer, call back a friend and then think, later, that I must have sounded rushed and unfriendly when that's not how I felt at all. I fax the mail, scissor open instant meals, answer the phone while wiping off the breakfast table.

I don't spent a meditative moment really tasting the blackberry jam or gazing at the faces of my sleeping children or stepping out to the porch to feel the rain on my face.

Or, if I do, I do it quickly, checking it off the list: Gazed at sleeping children. Lifted face to rain. Note to self: Smell roses tomorrow.

And I'm not alone. Everybody's life has speeded up. People used to spend months lolling on ocean liners just getting to Europe, or three or four hours in a carriage, smelling the green fields while getting to town. Now we prowl supermarket aisles in search of minute meals, send e-mails to friends instead of letters, rinse out pantyhose while we're in the shower, and wear jogging gear to the manicurist so we can take a twenty-minute run while our nails dry.

One woman told me, "I live by lists and scribbled notes on little yellow Post-Its stuck around my house and even in my car. My home is always messy, the clean laundry is always heaped on the ping-pong table waiting to be folded and put away, the yard is filled with weeds, and I make dinner quickly and leave it on the kitchen counter for my kids and husband to eat whenever they're home and passing through the kitchen. I wonder what I'm hurrying for."

We work hard even at our leisure, taking cruises that promise to leave us physically drained at the end of each day or replete with new lore from a day-long seminar.

Where, in all this hurry, do we find the quiet satisfactions of daily life that we once took for granted? When we do stop *doing* and start *being?*

One day, feeling overwhelmed, I asked readers of my *San Francisco Chronicle* column: What do you do? What's your version of hanging out the wash? The question seemed to touch a chord. Within days I had a large basket overflowing with hundreds of moments from other people's lives, people writing in to share the ways of slowing down they had discovered.

For a lot of people slowing down means getting their hands on something. They write letters in longhand though they have computers, wash dishes though they have dishwashers. One woman rubs leather shoes with mink oil until they shine, while thinking of the places the shoes have taken her. Another fired her psychiatrist because he laughed when she said she loved to iron. A third goes into the garden just for the sensual pleasure of pulling weeds from the dirt and breathing in the tangy odor. They plant camellia bushes, dance with the kitchen towel, or shovel the driveway while the snowblower sits in the garage.

For others, it means not just looking, but seeing. Some stray out to the yard, at night or first thing in the morning, to look at the sky and breathe the air. Others will spend a day following the light around the house.

A third group takes time for moments of stillness. They arrive early for doctors' appointments or refuse to use the car on Sundays. A mother decides to wait in the car during her son's guitar lesson rather than try to hit the bank, gas station, post office, and supermarket and be back in an hour. A woman with grown grandchildren finally found time to watch a leaf fall all the way from the tree to the ground.

Others, like me, are just learning how, just beginning to sample the powerful religion of ordinary life, of freshly mopped floors and stacked dishes and clothes blowing on the line. I am starting to understand that I can reclaim time, slow it down to the tempo I knew in childhood, by getting my hands on things. When this mood comes over me, I find myself wandering out to the back yard to pull weeds and pluck tired blossoms off the flowers. I wash a load of whites so I can fold the T-shirts, hot from the dryer, or call the dog out to the porch for a brushing. When even this isn't enough, I head to the kitchen to dig out my old ceramic blue bread pan and see if we have any yeast. I dump the dough onto a board, and then knead it, turning it over and over with my hands, adding more flour wherever it's sticky. Punching it down as the yeast activates and starts to fight back. A bread machine would do this for me, but then I would miss the way using my hands releases my mind, and suddenly I float into the present moment, with no mistakes behind me, no worries ahead of me.

The way to slow down in a hectic world is not to find even more ways of saving time, but to look for ways to spend it. Nowadays when I take a few minutes to step onto the porch in the morning with my coffee—which I've started to do now that I've been reminded to—I feel that all over the country people are stepping out with me, settling down on the step and listening to the birds and the rhythm of their own hearts.

Here are their stories and suggestions.

living an extraordinary **ordinary** life

Leave the office at lunch every day—even if all you do is go get a sandwich to bring back. It's not healthy to sit inside all day—get out and enjoy some fresh air and sunshine!

Live with someone who stops to smell the roses.

Find a room in your house with an interesting shape or lots of doors and windows. Lie with your back on the floor and your legs up against the wall. Look up and imagine that the world is really upside down.

If the TV breaks, don't fix it.

Start reading the weather page. Be sure to go out to the beach when the tides are extra low.

Learn to play the trumpet.

Borrow a small child and follow him or her around for a while—you'll notice things you haven't seen in years.

Teach your kids to play chess.

Read a nineteenth-century novel—the prose and descriptive passages will remind you of what you're not seeing and feeling in modern life.

Write letters to favorite people with a favorite pen.

Be sure to step outside when there is a new or full moon. See how much brighter the stars are on new moon nights? Draw a picture of the moon each day for twenty-eight days. You'll be surprised at what you learn.

Take a trip to the Midwest. If you live in the Midwest, travel to the South.

By
Hand

Doing work which has to be done over and over again helps us recognize the natural cycles of growth and decay, of birth and death, and thus become aware of the dynamic order of the universe. "Ordinary" work, as the root meaning of the word indicates, is work that is in harmony with the order we perceive in the natural environment.

—*Fritjof Capra*

It is not the years in your life but the life in your years that counts.

—*Adlai Stevenson*

the secret to slowing down to enrich your life is simple: Do something for which you have a proven, genetic lack of ability. Get in over your head immediately so you can't back out. These are easy rules, considering the benefits.

I remember discovering this. It was New Year's Eve, and I was fixing my car's alternator. I wrenched it out of the car, opened it up on the kitchen table, and saw coils and coils of colored wire.

In the three weeks it took me to do a fifty-minute job, I was forced to rein myself in, breathe slowly, and be patient—haste would have meant disaster. Since then, I've taken two months to paint a room, did a thirty-minute plumbing job in a weekend (the memory of which still pains my landlord), and spent a bit more than a year on a car project that would take a mechanic six hours. The outcome of each job ranged from not bad to catastrophic, but each one shifted my sense of time and gave me a renewed appreciation for natural resources as I communed with inventors throughout history.

The most recent example came Sunday. I had lovely photos of Alaska and frames in odd sizes for which no precut glass could be found. I headed for the hardware store. I began at 2 P.M. and by 6 P.M. had six usable panes. There was glass all over the rug and on the cat and in my socks—an entire sheet reduced to polygon-shaped shards. Glass from sand, sand from rocks, rocks slowly worn away by the sea. For days after that I noticed the smoothness of glass, the even edges of the windows in my house, and remembered the crunch of sand between my toes at the beach.

It's necessary to do this sort of thing these days. Our high-speed technology doesn't just disconnect us from our sensory world. It also disconnects us from our humility.

Don't overdo it, of course. Get help for things like hip-replacement surgery. There's a difference between humility and humiliation.

Celebrate the happiness that friends are always giving,
make every day a holiday and celebrate just living!

—*Amanda Bradley*

I work a pre-dawn shift, have a teenager in the throes of hormonal blast-off, another child snarling at the brink of puberty, and a husband I cherish.

But in the middle of my overscheduled, overburdened life, I get together with the most wonderful friend a person could ask for. We met years ago, when I was in my early twenties and she in her early seventies. She brought to my life a bright laugh, the soothing rhythm of her grandfather clock, and a gift I will use the rest of my life: She taught me to make quilts.

Using antique patterns kept in an old shoebox and scraps of fabric, some old, some new, she has taught me to love color and texture and design. We share ideas and fabric over lunch, and in her company I learn to take pride in a good strong seam or a quilt for a new baby.

The time I spend with her is limited, but when I bring my quilt pieces home, she is with me still. With each tiny stitch I hold together the pieces that make up my life.

The true way to render ourselves happy is to love our work and find in it our pleasure.

—*Francoise de Motteville*

I'm a window cleaner and I get very attached to the windows I work on. I know their individual personalities, their mineral deposits, bad seals, and BB holes. I remove every speck of bee gunk, snail trail, fly crud, and bird doo that desecrates "my" windows, as well as the damage inflicted by that natural enemy, the painter. I bring garden clippers and prune bushes and plants that dare to interfere with my windows. As I drive my route, I get great enjoyment from seeing my glass glistening in the sunlight.

If I am incapable of washing dishes joyfully, if I want to finish them quickly so I can go and have dessert, I will be equally incapable of enjoying my dessert. With the fork in my hand, I will be thinking about what to do next, and the texture and flavor of the dessert, together with the pleasure of eating it, will be lost. I will always be dragged into the future, never able to live in the present moment.

—*Thich Nhat Hanh*

Some women want their husbands to help do dishes after the evening meal. I only want my husband to bring dishes over from the table, then he can be on his way to watch TV or read the paper, because the next half hour or forty-five minutes is all mine. Yes, I have a dishwasher, but while I wash the pots and pans or clean the stovetop and counters, I'm collecting my thoughts, thinking through troubling problems, brainstorming ideas for a short story, or just letting my mind wander.

> We are the living links in a life force that moves and plays through and around us, binding the deepest soils with the farthest stars.
>
> —*Alan Chadwick*

I'm a Norwegian immigrant. I came to America with my wife when I was twenty-one. When we left Oslo in 1964, with $900 to our name, we never dreamed we wouldn't go back, but scholarships, job offers, and business opportunities have kept us here.

The past thirty-seven years have been extremely rewarding. Starting from scratch—no family, no friends, speaking a foreign language—was all very difficult, but my wife and I worked together. She put me through graduate school by working as a secretary, and I played Mr. Mom to our children while studying for a Ph.D. I currently own a small engineering firm that employs twenty people.

My life as I describe it now sounds like the American dream, and in many ways it has been. But with the dream have come my share of nightmares. There have been problems with employees, times when business has been slow, and, a few years ago, a lawsuit with a Japanese company. There have been outrageous attorney bills and court decisions, sleepless nights, and canceled vacations. Raising two daughters has also proved trying at times.

When things get tough, I water the lawn and hose down the driveway. I know this might sound strange, but it's actually very relaxing. Standing outside in whatever I happen to be wearing that day, I water away and think. The water puts me in a trance and I focus completely. As the grass gets wet, I feel better. As the dirt on the pavement washes away into the gutter leaving the area clean, I feel in control.

I have been known to stand outside for hours at a time, watering away my worries.

Gratitude is the memory of the heart; therefore forget not to say often, I have all I ever enjoyed.

—*Lydia Child*

We have a great wood-burning stove, and most winter days the heat never comes on. There's something elemental about getting wood delivered, stacking it, hauling it in, and building a fire. It takes involvement. Logs have to be added during the evening. Your hands get dirty. It's real. And, it's also a great way to get the house toasty without huge heating bills.

Millions of persons long for immortality who do not know what to do with themselves on a rainy afternoon.

—*Susan Ertz*

I can't cook. Because I'm a woman and "supposed" to know how, I've decided to be horrible at it. Some weekends, though, I'm overcome by the desire to prepare a meal. A great meal.

I take all day. I imagine what the perfect meal would be— fresh, organic vegetables, wonderfully ripe fruit, a beautiful salad, maybe a light pasta, some freshly caught seafood . . . whatever. Then I plan my route. My favorite cheese shop is always a stop; I'll ask the man at the counter, "What do you recommend?" and he'll give me a taste of a new cheese from Denmark or Provence that makes me swoon, and I'll buy it.

Next I stop by the bakery. Usually a baguette is the perfect accoutrement to go with my cheese, and right on the spot I eat part of it to get me through the rest of my strenuous day. Then I go to my favorite corner produce stand and the health-food store. I load up on veggies and fruit, imagining all of the salads and succulent fruits that I'll dine on. And finally I stop and buy a bottle of wine. A good merlot.

When I get home I unpack my groceries. I open the wine. I slice up my baguette and spread on the ripe cheese. I cut up my cantaloupe and garnish it with strawberries and purple grapes. The little organic pear-shaped tomatoes, along with an avocado, are thrown onto some crisp lettuce and then lightly misted with oil and vinegar, salt and pepper. And then I take my delectables to the couch, where my favorite book is waiting, and eat.

The soul should always stand ajar, ready to welcome the ecstatic experience.

—Emily Dickinson

the joy when nursing an infant of feeling the soft, warm, almost moist little hands butterflying on one's breast and knowing that right then to that one human being you are essential—that is happiness.

One of my heroes, a Swedish writer named Gunnar Ekelof (whom, if he had written in a major language, we would all study in school), writes that every human being is allowed 180 seconds of pure and unmitigated happiness—not 180 seconds at once, but 180 seconds total in our lives.

If he's right, I have gotten more than my share. With each of my children I have experienced more than 180 seconds of the pure happiness where every instinct, every reason, every rational thought, and every irrational emotion work together in a glorious whole.

If we had a keen vision of all ordinary life, it would be like hearing the grass grow or the squirrel's heart beat, and we should die of the roar which lies on the other side of silence. As it is, the quickest of us walk about well-wadded with stupidity.

—George Eliot

I read somewhere that a tribe of Americans-who-came-wandering-in-about-forty-thousand-years-ago had small pouches in which they kept fragrance memories. When anything remarkable happened, they would pick a plant or collect some pebbles to save. When they wanted to recreate that memory, they would take out the talisman.

For me the smell of laundry drying in the breeze is one, as is the smell of barbecued ribs in the oven on Saturdays. Irresistible!

I always saw better when my eyes were closed.

—*Tom Waits*

I was introduced to golf at a very early age by a father who had a quiet reverence for the game. I can remember being about six, standing by my father on the first tee as the last mist of morning lifted off the fairways, standing very still and quiet looking out at the beautiful expanses of undulating grass and stately trees and knowing that nothing could possibly be more beautiful. It was so powerfully peaceful.

Despite the sound tutoring I received, I went through the typical golf growing pains—wanting to smash the ball into outer space, swinging so hard I nearly came out of my shoes, becoming angry and frustrated by the all-too-frequent errant shot. I gave up. But then, at a time in my life when everything seemed to be moving too quickly with too much pressure attached to it, I rediscovered the game of golf and it's been my salvation.

For me, golf is a meditation in peaceful relaxation. I know that to many of the golfers I see hacking and cursing their way around a course this must sound odd, but it is precisely how I experience it. At the heart of this paradox is the golf swing. It actually punishes excess exertion of energy and demands that you stop trying so damned hard and simply (and I mean simply) swing the club slowly and smoothly. The harder and faster you swing, the more likely your shot will dribble forward or shoot off in some unintended direction. The more slowly, more peaceful, more calmly contained your swing, the greater the odds of smacking the ball sweetly down the middle of the fairway.

When I play, progressively, with each shot, I go more slowly; I swing within myself in a calm, even rhythm. Between shots, I've gotten into the habit of quietly breathing in the extraordinary surrounding beauty. By the end of a round, I'm as relaxed and peaceful as a monk on a mountaintop.

So powerful is the experience that I don't even have to play golf to benefit. When time is short, hitting a bucket of balls at the driving range is almost as effective. In a pinch, just holding a golf club in my hands—feeling the grip, standing over an imaginary ball—will be enough to bring me back to that wonderful place of centered calm. Once, ascending in a high-speed elevator to a very important meeting, I closed my eyes, put my hands together in a classic interlocking grip, and stood over an imaginary golf ball in order to calm my nerves. When I opened my eyes, standing at the open elevator door was the executive I had come to meet with. He smiled and said, "Now that's the way to ride an elevator."

If of thy mortal goods thou art bereft.

And from thy slender store

Two loaves alone to thee are left,

Sell one, and with the dole

Buy hyacinths to feed thy soul!

—*Persian poet, c. 1300*

I discovered the joy of working with my hands after I turned thirty. My wife and I opened a card and gift shop about eight years ago so that we could pursue our hobby of letterpress printing using hand-set type and hand-driven presses. I still get a thrill when I open the door each morning and smell the mixture of old wood, ink, paper, and a hint of oil. I don't have to shout over the din of automatic presses. And I have classical music playing most of the time.

The first thing most men say when they see me working with a hand press is, "You can put a motor on that, you know. Go a lot faster. Make more money."

Yes, I'd make more money, but I'd lose so much *pleasure*.

One day a young woman I had printed some letterhead for came in to reorder five hundred more. I told her she could take the one I had printed to the quick print shop down the street and get the job done for less than half of what it would cost to have it done by hand.

She thanked me and left. Ten minutes later she came back. "I don't care how much more it costs or how long it takes, I want you to do it. It's so noisy and chaotic down there, and so nice and peaceful here."

You can't get spoiled if you do your own ironing.

—*Meryl Streep*

I love vacuuming. Vacuuming marks a path and covers the ground. You see the entire pattern—you see where you've been and where you're going. Try sprinkling some deodorant powder about. Utter satisfaction. Or try more advanced vacuuming: creating new patterns, finding the most efficient, the most serpentine. Try to vacuum the entire room without crossing any previously vacuumed paths. Vacuum the kitchen linoleum. Take a small portable with a wide attachment and vacuum a placid cat. Remove the attachment and see if the hose will suck onto your forearm (be careful not to leave it on for any length of time unless you want a hickey). Vacuum your car and discover lost treasure.

Unfortunately, my current home has hardwood floors. I'm looking to move.

We shall not cease from exploration and the end of all our exploring will be to arrive where we started and know the place for the first time.

—*T. S. Eliot*

I have discovered that when I remove clothes from the dryer, if I fold them carefully, press them with my hands to make sharp creases, and stack them in neat piles, I receive enormous satisfaction.

It is good to have an end to journey toward; but it is the journey that matters, in the end.

—*Ursula K. LeGuin*

Weeding! I go out and get down on my knees among the rosebushes and attack the oxalis. Of course it always comes back, but how satisfying to dig it out by the roots and toss it into the bucket! It's great stress therapy: Dig with the right hand, grab and toss with the left. My shoulder always aches afterward, so I get my husband to massage it and double the pleasure!

To love oneself is the beginning of a lifelong romance.

—*Oscar Wilde*

for me it's the act of chopping and skimming, the kitchen windows steaming up, and the room filling with the scent of chicken bones, whole heads of garlic, great lifeboats of carrots, onions, and celery, and a gauze purse filled with parsley, black peppercorns, bay leaves, dried thyme, and oregano and tied up with string: the mysterious *bouquet garni*.

I finish with an essential product, but the real benefit has been time engaged with myself. Only a small part of my mind has been occupied, and the rest is free to wander where it will. It is the last bastion, as my back injury has wiped out my former activities: woolgathering, gardening, running, and long drives. They all required some kind of intact frame, and I am rickety old scaffolding that collapses with the slightest breeze. Instead I have miniaturized my sense of wonder and have come to appreciate the glories of well-made stock and things that come to fruition slowly and lovingly.

In order *to do* it is necessary *to be*. And it is necessary first to understand what *to be* means.

—*P. D. Ouspensky*

a friend and I, along with several other women, started a quilting group. One woman dropped out because she said we talked too much, ate too much, and didn't sew enough.

Well, that's just it, isn't it?

The reward of patience is patience.

—*Saint Augustine*

I grew up in the 1950s. For someone who loved order and cleanliness and was as involved in community projects as my mother, we spent an inordinate amount of time going to the beach. For my mother, gaily waving her cigarette in the front of our red '56 Dodge, it was an easy hop over the hills to the ocean.

There wasn't a chore whose pleasurable side she couldn't find. The gentle hiss of an iron gliding across damp Irish linen was as visceral a pleasure to her as the sound of sand sucking the waves at the beach; a stack of freshly ironed linen neatly arranged in a drawer was as moving as a view of the Farallons on a clear day.

You have to sniff out joy. Keep your nose to the joy trail.

—Buffy Sainte-Marie

dusting the sewing table my great-great-grandfather made for my grandma, the Victorian table my great-grandmother dusted, and the tacky, tacky frame my best friend sent me with a picture of the two of us down at the beach. Dusting the 1950s rooster lamp that I bought on sale at Woolworth's for $2.99 and carried home on the bus. Dusting the furniture my husband made for me.

You only live once—but if you work it right, once is enough.

—*Joe E. Louis*

In the winter I shovel snow. I stand with the snowflakes falling on my bare head, sometimes at two in the morning when the rest of the world is asleep, sometimes at two in the afternoon when the birds are screeching for more seed in their feeder and the boys are too loud for me inside the house. I shovel our entire driveway—knowing we could hire a plow, knowing the snowblower sits idle in the garage, knowing that soon the snow will be two inches deep again.

Live in the present,
Do all the things that need to be done.
Do all the good you can each day.
The future will unfold.

—Peace Pilgrim

Whenever we couldn't find Mom, my brother and I knew she was down in the basement ironing, either running sheets through the Ironrite that Dad had given her for their anniversary or doing what she loved the best: pressing the intricate details on shirts and blouses, making them crisp and neat without the aid of spray starch.

She would be down there where it was cool, liberated for a while from her service to us, soothing herself the only way she knew how. Even slowing down had to be disguised as work— she could never justify doing nothing.

I learned that "I'll be up in a minute" was to buy her more time at her ironing board, surrounded by her equivalent of half-finished canvases and the smell of turpentine.

> The worst of all possible things is not to live in the physical world.
>
> —*Wallace Stevens*

I paint houses and refinish hardwood floors. Whenever I've finished re-sanding a floor, before I've sealed it with resins, I lie down on it and think about what might happen there. People will live and work and talk together; they'll argue and maybe fall in love.

What we do today, right now, will have an accumulated effect on all our tomorrows.

—Alexandra Stoddard

I do needlepoint. I make pillows and pictures for people I care about, my family and friends. Since I choose the project to suit a particular person, I think about that person and his or her life and our relationship as I work— sometimes for months. I made a memorial pillow for a friend whose teenaged daughter died accidentally. As I stitched, I thought about her brief life and cried a little for them both. I just finished a cat pillow for a friend who's moving to Chicago and leaving her college-age son for the first time. While I worked on her pillow I thought about the kind of person she is and what this move means in her life.

No day is so bad that it can't be fixed by a nap.

—*Carrie Snow*

On Saturdays I take the sheets and undies outside into the fresh air and hang them up in the sun and wind. No one else is allowed the job—I tell them it's because they don't know how to hang out clothes. I feel the early morning sun on my back and listen to quiet sounds as I leave the long week's raggedy days behind. I bathe in the morning light under the clothesline and delight in the feeling of air on my skin after being shut up in the office all week. Oh, yes, I have a dryer, but on nice days it sits silent. Placed on the bed, the fragrant sheets from the line become a silent welcome after a tiring day.

By losing present time, we lose all time.

—*W. Gurney Benham*

I remember reading a magazine that gave this advice to working mothers: Perform small chores while you're doing something else. Clean the bathroom while you bathe your children. Sew buttons on shirts while you talk on the phone. Clean out a drawer as you watch TV. I've gotten pretty good at this sort of thing—so much so that I hardly allow myself to even idle on the pot anymore. I keep a stack of self-improving reading there.

Then I read an article by a woman writer describing her failed marriage. She had stayed home baking pies and planning birthday parties. She said that her now-almost-grown son used one sentence to sum up what he remembered about his childhood: "You were always cleaning."

That stopped me cold. Even though I'm not a stay-at-home mom, I do spend a lot of time doing chore-related things. Do I want my four-year-old daughter Kara to remember only that about me years from now?

One day on vacation, Kara and I spent hours collecting and stacking rocks in front of our cottage in the warm sun. I remember that day more clearly and more fondly than the many days I have spent efficiently checking items off my lists.

I've begun to discover the satisfaction and pleasure in doing one thing at a time, of savoring little experiences. I know Kara is also much happier when my full attention is on *her* in the bathtub, and not on trying to get rid of that pesky ring around it.

Eternity has nothing to do with the hereafter.... This is it.... If you don't get it here, you won't get it anywhere. The experience of eternity right here and now is the function of life. Heaven is not the place to have the experience; here's the place to have the experience.

—*Joseph Campbell*

I do my best thinking while cleaning the toilet bowl. When I'm performing this mindless, distasteful task, I escape the monotony by daydreaming, reflecting, and fantasizing. I flush my mind.

It is eternity now. I am in the midst of it. It is about me in the sunshine.

—*Richard Jefferies*

every year the sitting area on my deck shrinks as I buy more pots and fill them with summer flowers. I water them slowly, pot by pot. Once in a while, I try to do two things at once—water and talk on the phone. But it's distracting to pay attention to the person at the other end while I'm watching the water flow into the rich brown soil and smiling at the flowers. So, by the beginning of July, I just let the phone ring when I'm watering.

As each plant soaks up the wet nourishment, I stand amidst the air, the smells, and the sounds of life, and all of them help to slow my world down, quiet my thoughts, and give me time to pause.

Now all my teachers are dead except silence.

—*W. S. Merwin*

When I was married and my daughter was still at home, it was folding clean laundry. Sorting clothes according to owner—John's here, Chelsea's there— then folding each piece. In particular, I liked folding John's underwear. It was an intimate, slightly sexual exercise, suitable for promoting thoughts of lovemaking. If he were traveling and I had nothing of his to fold, I felt his absence more sharply.

Through the years, I folded Chelsea's clothes as candy-striped Health-Tex T-shirts gave way to scoop-necked, body-hugging T-shirts from The Limited. I folded her underwear as it went from flowered cotton briefs to the skimpiest of bikinis, really no more than bits of lace strung on elastic. Undershirts gave way to slinky bras, ridiculous scraps that made me chuckle.

Now I am divorced and live alone in an apartment in the

city. I find myself frequenting the far end of a particular pier, where my only company is swooping gulls and diving cormorants. I watch the freighters making their way out to sea, and I still think about John and Chelsea, about things large or small, earth-shattering or mundane, but I think about them now from a different perspective: that of a middle-aged woman on her own.

And I think about how I miss John's and Chelsea's underwear tangled up with mine.

It is of no use walking anywhere to preach unless our walking is our preaching.

—*Saint Francis of Assisi*

now that I'm home on maternity leave, I have made it my personal mission to press my husband's shirts myself, a task that generally takes me an hour and a half (slow but thorough). This is my hour and a half per week to reflect, daydream, work out problems, plan ahead, and try to figure out who is the murderer in *Prime Suspect II*.

I make sure I will have this time to myself by ironing shirts after the kids are in bed and letting my answering machine pick up calls. God help the telemarketer who interrupts my weekly ironing session with a pitch to buy aluminum siding!

My husband is baffled by my desire to iron his shirts. This is the one time a week I can count on for myself. I'm thinking of investing in a sleeve board.

Getting and spending, we lay waste our powers.

—*Ralph Waldo Emerson*

I've been scanning the sales ads, thinking about getting a bread machine. Maybe if I wait awhile, I thought, I can get one cheaper. But then I remembered how I like to spank the dough to see if it's kneaded enough—as one book said, it should feel like a baby's bottom. That thought reminds me how connected I feel to countless generations of women who have made bread for their families, and how much I love the smell of bread baking.

I wonder how it would feel for that bread to come from a machine into which I dump ingredients in the rush of doing something else, then punch in the correct time-delay sequence. No more thinking of all the women who have made bread before me; no more smacking it to see if it feels like a baby's bottom.

On second thought, I think I'll keep the flour on the floor, the overactive yeast oozing out of the cup, and the awkward tiptoe position I have to assume to knead the bread on a counter that's too high. I'll keep it all, happily.

> Freedom means choosing your burden.
>
> *—Hephzibah Menuhin*

I have a confession to make that I hope my father never hears—I love weeding. When I was a small boy, my father used to pay me fifty cents an hour to pull weeds from our extensive gardens. I suppose, looking back on my wage scale, it was a great deal for him, but it was even better for me. It was such a feeling of accomplishment to finish a square area and look down at all that sweet-smelling moist dirt and not see a single little invader.

Blessed with more garden space than one boy could keep weed-free, it seemed at the time a source of unlimited riches—all for doing what was fun to do in the first place. One particularly ambitious summer, I used to set my alarm clock for sunrise in order to give myself time to weed away the morning hours and still leave plenty of time for more normal summer activities. At the tender age of ten, I planted a vegetable garden that covered nearly a quarter acre of land and worked diligently every day, weeding and playing Panama Canal with my extensive series of irrigation ditches.

All that training has conditioned me so strongly that now all I need to do to return to childlike mental health is plant myself in the garden. It must sound truly corny, but what a great way to get grounded—on your hands and knees in the dirt, face down, all attention focused on seeking out unwanted little weeds.

> Perfection consists not in doing extraordinary things, but in doing ordinary things extraordinarily well.
>
> —*Angelique Arnauld*

Once a week or so I buy flowers at the grocery store and take great pleasure in arranging that fresh bunch of flowers in a vase or two.

The other day at the store, one bunch of particularly vibrant dark pinks was much thicker than usual. I just had to buy it—pinching pennies can be so satisfying! Later, I spent twenty minutes at my house happily making one arrangement after another, filling vase after vase. The florist had counted a few too many blooms into the rubber-banded bunch and given me a bargain both satisfying and beautiful.

living an extraordinary **ordinary** life

Pick fresh fruit.

Take ten minutes to recall a pleasant memory (perhaps by looking at old photos). You need your memories during the hard times.

Be kind to the first person you run into in the morning in the outside world.

Try to do something each week, something repetitive that changes a little, like watching the same tree change with the seasons.

Leave your watch off.

Subscribe to "Star Date" from the McDonald Observatory in Texas. It will tell you what to look for in the night sky.

Take your child on a flower walk, sniffing every flower along the way.

Have a weekly "family home evening" like the Mormons do: All family members spend the evening going to a movie together, playing a game at home, preparing a special dinner, or just reading in the same room.

Send someone a postcard when they aren't expecting it.

Sit and do nothing for five minutes. Just five minutes.

Notice colors—they're everywhere.

Instead of speeding through the preparation of a meal, decide that dinner will be a few minutes later. Wrap your hand around your child's hand and show her how to cut fresh mushrooms or grate cheese.

Give up just one labor-saving device in your household.

Build a fire in the fireplace and just watch the flames.

Seeing
Deeply

The moment one gives close attention to anything, even a blade of grass, it becomes a mysterious, awesome, indescribably magnificent world in itself.

—*Henry Miller*

We don't see things as they are, we see them as we are.

—*Anaïs Nin*

Yesterday on my way home from work, standing on a crowded train with tired-looking people, I began to panic. Nobody was speaking. Nobody was smiling. We were all bad animal cliches—either rats from the rat race or passive cows being herded. Suddenly, my life as a single woman seemed painfully mundane and my personality devoid of any personhood.

Rushing home, I found myself searching for a way to make myself feel alive. Ice cream would be only a superficial solution. Calling all of my friends would put off dealing with my abysmal feelings only temporarily. I didn't think I could concentrate enough to read.

Then I remembered what I could do. After putting on comfortable sweats, I went to the living room and grabbed my photo albums, all three of them, that represent practically every major stage of my life. This ritual is always the same. I start at the beginning. Me, a small baby, being held by doting parents and relatives. Me, cute young child, swinging a whiffle bat. Me, my brother, and best friend learning to ride bikes. Me going to my first dance. Me with my first boyfriend who was on my baseball team. Me going off to college. Me on vacation with my girlfriends.

Somehow, seeing my life spread out in a photo album, I can ground myself. I feel the events that have shaped me, the people who have loved and supported me, the places that hold precious memories—and I can come back to myself.

If you take a flower in your hand and really look at it, it's your world for the moment.

—*Georgia O'Keeffe*

I take time all day long to find rainbows. I got a great one this morning. A woman came to our business dressed in a magenta jogging suit with a blinding red raincoat over it. She brought a large piece of needlepoint. It would go on a French chair and needed just the right pale velvet for trim. We both gazed at it with pleasure: antique petit point with animals and flowers. A rainbow.

Life is what happens to you while you're busy making other plans.

—*John Lennon*

One of my great passions is birdwatching. Once I was on a business trip to South Florida and arranged to have an extra day to get out into the Everglades. I was very excited, having never been there before. I stayed in a motel near the entrance to the Everglades and had planned my day with the precision of a military invasion: get up at 4 A.M., drive to wooded area for owls, be at nearby marshy area at dawn, 6:30 to 7:30 search for bird *X,* and so on, through my departure from the airport that evening.

At 3:59, before the alarm could ring, I jumped out of bed, threw my stuff into the car, stuffed my room key through the night slot, locked my keys in the trunk, and jumped into the car. That's when I realized that I had no keys and no trunk release and nothing was open. At 4:03, in a state of panic, I called a locksmith who said he'd be by in an hour or so.

Deep depression was followed a few minutes later by

peaceful surrender. "Slow down, relax," whispered the world. "Enjoy where you are right now." So I sat on the hood of the car, watching the stars disappear and the early glow of dawn. Two hours later the locksmith appeared, and I cruised out to the Everglades for a wonderful day. Refreshed, I made my flight in plenty of time.

The only thing you have to offer another human being, ever, is your own state of being.

—*Ram Dass*

each time I take the bread and wine in our church service, I kneel down, think of my sweet wife, Ann, and my daughters, Leigh, Sarah, and Jessica, by name. I see my grandchildren and their fathers. I sense my deceased mother and father. I think of the Kennedys, King, Gandhi, Luther, Lincoln, and Jesus. In the sacrament I feel tied to my family and my history. I am calm, reflective, and peaceful.

Tell me what you pay attention to and I will tell you who you are.

—*José Ortega y Gasset*

I spend the morning at a coffee shop reading the paper, then practically float out of there on the buzz of the strong coffee. Then I head down to the Palace of Fine Arts with a bottle of Walgreen's bubbles. Sitting in the sun under a tree, with an apple or a great book in one hand, I blow bubbles into the sky—watching them float into the blue, hearing the shout of "Bubbles!" from the children, seeing the old folks smile as they watch from their benches, and the teenaged skateboarder who's much too cool to smile, but is the first to ask if he can blow some too.

This is not a dress rehearsal. This is it.

—*Tom Cunningham*

I 've discovered that the real truth is if you are paying attention—and it is, as the Buddhists say, *right* attention—then any and every moment, no matter what you are doing, is so full of richness and wonder that nothing else matters.

Live all you can; it's a mistake not to. It doesn't so much matter what you do in particular, so long as you have your life. If you haven't had that what *have* you had?

—*Henry James*

When I'm walking home, my head still full of problems with my boss, I try not to let myself get all the way there without noticing it's a crisp winter day and that it's a pleasure to be striding along in a warm coat, watching the sun set the windows of the city on fire. I stop and sit for a while on a bench, listening to the shouts of kids playing basketball in the fading light, and feel my spirits rise, simply from having paid attention.

I only have to take up this or that to flood my soul with memories.

—*Dorothee DeLuzy*

We have several pieces of art (paintings, handmade bowls, dried flower arrangements) made by friends. Sometimes I just take the "house tour" and look at them and think of the people who made them. This often brings back memories of my friends more vivid than if I were looking at pictures of them.

> Inside yourself or outside, you never have to change what you see, only the way you see it.
>
> —*Thaddeus Golas*

I became a birdwatcher a few years ago because it eased the constant belching I experienced during six months of chemotherapy. At thirty-nine, I was told by my doctor that an innocent little breast lump had a few cancer cells in it after all. Suddenly I had eight months of cancer treatment ahead of me, and working tumbled way down the list of priorities.

I started taking long walks and found myself not watching my feet, or even thinking about much of anything, but looking up, and there they were, these wonderful fellow creatures to keep me company, soaring and singing and gliding. One night I even took flight in my dreams for the first time in more than three decades.

The cancer treatment is now behind me, and I used that time of self-examination well, I think. I tell the ones I love that

I love them, slowly, clearly, and often. I still work hard, but with nice people who send me home when I look tired, and sometimes even when I don't. I make less money, but I give away more of it, and try to be kind.

My soul can find no staircase to heaven unless it be through earth's loveliness.

—*Michelangelo*

We make an earnest effort to compost our kitchen waste, specifically coffee grounds, chopped-up banana skins, apple cores, and other biodegradable gunk. As the compost heap is at the very back of our yard, every morning after breakfast I wander out with a cutting board full of goodies for the little red worms. This trip necessitates a journey through the garden, and that means a step into sloweddown time.

There's always something new poking up through the adobe, or starting to leaf or bloom, or growing where it shouldn't, or even just rimmed picturesquely with frost. For a gardener—even a hit-or-miss one like me—a walk through one's own garden is almost guaranteed to provide a meditative change of pace.

The voyage of discovery lies not in finding new landscapes, but in having new eyes.

—*Marcel Proust*

I find moments of tranquility by looking out my front window, which has a lovely northern view. I try to embrace the moment between daylight and twilight that turns the sky into a lovely, gentle spectrum of reds, purples, and blues. One by one, the streets are defined in front of me by the glow of lights that become brighter as the day leaves me behind.

We ourselves cannot put any magic spells on this world. The world is its own magic.

—*Suzuki Roshi*

a few weeks ago, after twenty-one days of rain, I was walking home from work with my hat and overcoat on. It took me about ten minutes to realize not only that it was not raining, but that there was a soft breeze blowing along the avenue and the sky was a vibrant orange from the setting sun. I rushed to my house, peeled off the layers, and grabbed the nearest animal, which happened to be my cat. I put a makeshift leash on her and we went for a walk. I can't speak for my cat, but I was so moved by the experience that when I came back my husband looked at me and the cat on the leash and asked if we were okay.

A very merry, dancing, drinking,
Laughing, quaffing, and unthinking time.

—John Dryden

I have a small collection of wines, and sometimes I'll just go over the list or go down to the basement and look at them. They remind me of trips to wineries on hot summer days, wine tasting with friends, and special dinners with my wife. I notice wines I'm saving for people I'm going to see, and wines I've shared with people in the past.

A change in the weather is enough to renew the world and ourselves.

—*Marcel Proust*

When my husband is away, I sometimes spend the night in the guest bedroom in the old-fashioned double bed I used before I was married. It has a fluffy comforter, ruffled pillow shams, and pretty sheets. If I adjust the blinds just right, I get a lovely view of the treetops and city lights, instead of the tar-and-gravel rooftops and power lines I see during the day. And because there is only one outlet in the room, just enough for a lamp and a clock, I read in bed rather than watch TV. Spending the night in the guest room makes me feel as though I'm staying at a bed and breakfast inn.

It takes a golden ear to be empty enough of itself to hear clearly.

—*M. C. Richards*

ight will fall on something, say, a pink peony petal in an otherwise shaded garden, and it will capture me and deliver me from myself—from my worries about money, about being HIV positive, and the dog needing a bath. It often seems to happen when I should have been somewhere ten minutes ago.

Perhaps because of the electrification of the planet, natural night light is the sweetest. In the villages of Nepal the stars are so bright they tinge the edges of gambos leaves with a soft glow. And in Sri Lanka, Venus is strong enough to cast palm leaf shadows on the sand.

It is life near the bone, where it is sweeter.

—*Henry David Thoreau*

When I first lived with my love, I enjoyed looking at his underwear hanging next to mine. When I saw our pants side by side I thought of us walking together. After a very passionate night, I took a laundry pen and marked a heart on the sheet so I could think of that night each time I hung it to dry.

> When we pay attention, whatever we are doing—whether it be cooking, cleaning or making love—is transformed.... We begin to notice details and textures that we never noticed before; everyday life becomes clearer, sharper, and at the same time more spacious.
>
> —*Rick Fields*

I used to be a remarkably fast eater. I read or watched television while eating. I still do that during some meals.

On most days, though, I eat my breakfast cereal very slowly, and remember to bow to the bowl before each spoonful. Also, I bow to my water glass before each drink. I try to make the bow a slow one: I try to hold it for a beat and then breathe slowly and deeply when coming out of it.

During that bow and while eating I try to think of all the sacrifices and hard work that have gone into making this food. I try to visualize the farms in Iowa and orchards in California where it was grown, the people working there and what exactly they do, the clerks who put it on the store shelves, the clerk who sold it to me. I think about what I will do with the life the food gives me.

If you wait for tomorrow, tomorrow comes. If you don't wait for tomorrow, tomorrow comes.

—*Senegalese proverb*

Several years ago I took a trip across America on my bicycle—5,000 miles' worth. I was forty-one years old and had never considered myself much of an athlete. As I rode slowly and contemplatively across this land, I learned a lot about my body rhythms. I learned that I was capable of so much more than I had ever imagined. The only days that were difficult were those for which I was not mentally prepared. A mountain pass was easy if I knew it was coming, but a little bump in the road could become a major curse if it took me by surprise. I learned that it is far superior to see less but to see it well. On a bike, you don't just see: You absorb with all your senses the smells, tastes, sounds, and feelings as you travel along the road.

Today I try to live my life much more deliberately. I earn less money and do less work than before, but I have more time.

We do not remember days, we remember moments.

—*Cesare Pavese*

my kids were in the preschool "Mommy, Mommy, Mommy" phase, and I was working daily and driving excessively. As I stood at the kitchen sink washing dishes one day, I looked out the window and was shocked to notice the sky. It was bright pink and purple. I thought, "Carla, you never take the time to just sit and watch the sunset." So I went out to the backyard with my yellow rubber gloves on and for ten minutes gazed at those celestial colors.

Unfortunately, I forgot to turn off the water in the plugged-up sink and returned to a flooded kitchen just as my husband pulled into the driveway. But it was worth it!

Now when I need those quiet moments, I check the faucets, turn off the phone, and go outside to stare at the sky. It's big, it's free, it's miraculous!

We have first raised a dust and then complain we cannot see.

—*Bishop George Berkeley*

I used to drive, but now I take the bus everywhere. From a bus window, I take in everything, the buildings and the people, on a human scale and on their own terms. I see the world from a slower, bus-stop-to-bus-stop pace, and not from a freeway off-ramp while doing forty-five miles an hour. I see polished Victorians and smell the kitchens of Chinatown and North Beach. I hear snatches of conversation, I see people drinking espresso on the way to work, and, watching, I become part of the fabric of the city.

The true harvest of my daily life is somewhat as intangible and indescribable as the tints of morning or evening. It is a little star-dust caught, a segment of the rainbow which I have clutched.

—*Henry David Thoreau*

my current schedule requires me to get up earlier than my wife and our two-year-old daughter. I may grumble when the alarm goes off, but I relish that hour of solitude. It's not just sitting at the table, drinking coffee and reading the paper in silence. Nor is it the beauty of the morning. What I love is seeing the remains of yesterday's activities and dramas: the stuffed animal wrapped in a dishtowel "blanket" on the chair where we left it last night, the last crackling cinders in the fireplace, a little sock lying under the table. It's sort of an archaeology of the living. I see the object, and it brings a flood of memories.

We want our minds to be clear—not so we can think clearly, but so we can be open in our perceptions.

—*M. C. Richards*

In the car, while waiting for one or another of the kids, I lean back in the seat and take deep breaths and look out the window at the world. I notice the sun or the rain and the other people rushing about, or I put on a favorite tape and sing at the top of my lungs.

Some things ... arrive on their own mysterious hour, on their own terms and not yours, to be seized or relinquished forever..

—*Gail Godwin*

On a hot summer day in 1990, I almost missed the only total eclipse of the sun that will occur in my lifetime.

Oh, I knew it was happening. In fact I was frantic about making sure I saw it. I pushed pins through cardboard to make tiny holes to project the sun's image on a piece of white paper. I borrowed a friend's welding mask and tried to look at the sun directly.

Satisfied that I had experienced the phenomenon, I picked up the kids at preschool. When I drove the car into our cool, dark barn and stepped out, I saw all over the floor and walls tiny sun shapes with big bites the moon had taken out of them. A hundred years of woodpeckers had made perfect openings for the sun to project itself through and show us what we'd been looking for.

Time goes, you say? Ah no!
Alas, Time stays, *we* go.

—*Austin Dobson*

I 'm one of those men who for better or for worse (and it's probably both) gets completely immersed in my work. The downside is that big chunks of time can go by without my even noticing that the rest of my life is aimlessly drifting and that my body is being worn down and my neck is scrunched up in constant pain. By the time I realize how wound up I've become, it takes some serious unwinding to get me back into halfway human form.

By far the best way for me to accomplish this is by watching baseball—not just any TV baseball, but daytime, stolen hours, middle-of-the-week, ballpark baseball. I live in the San Francisco Bay Area, and I never really thought about how much I have come to depend on this ritual until the year when the Giants were "sold" to St. Petersburg, Florida. It resulted in an almost palpable panic as I realized that the one sure method

I had for reducing my tension level was about to disappear forever. So their staying was a great relief.

The magic begins to work the moment I decide to go to a ballgame. I almost never plan ahead; the feeling just overtakes me and I know that I am not going to work: I'm heading to the ballpark. Almost immediately I start to feel a childlike glee, exactly like I did on those rare occasions when I missed school as a kid—I'm playing hooky and it feels great.

I usually start off in the morning just like I was going to work, but instead head to a cafe and leisurely eat a big greasy breakfast. Then I drive to the ballpark and arrive early enough to sit quietly in the stands, read the morning paper front to back, and watch the pre-game rituals.

That in itself is a great exercise in relaxation. Baseball is unlike any other sport; more about timing and pacing than strength and quickness—even the pre-game rituals have an almost fluid pace to them. Fielding practice unfolds slowly with a coach tossing up and hitting balls to players who move in and out of the different positions in a seemingly random fashion. All the while everyone seems almost as interested in joking around with each other as in catching the ball.

Other players are scattered around the field, stretching, doing slow wind sprints, or just clumped in groups shooting the breeze. When batting practice comes around, the players again move in and out of the batting cage seemingly randomly, joking with teammates and producing the languid melody of a wooden bat smacking a pitched baseball.

Meanwhile the stands slowly come alive. Ushers and early arrivals have plenty of time to talk baseball, reliving the recent games, commenting on the mysterious twists of fate that seem to make up so much of the texture of the game. It's like being in a familiar neighborhood—I know all these people even though I don't know them; we are a community.

As game time approaches, an odd kind of tension begins to grow. Odd because although it can be easily felt, it doesn't seem like tension at all: the conference at home plate, where the managers exchange line-up cards and have a brief meeting with the umpires; then a lull followed by a burst of activity as the home team runs out of the dugout and onto the field to take their positions. It always amazes me how such seemingly casual preparations unfolding in such a seemingly unhurried pace result in the first pitch crossing the plate at precisely the scheduled starting time.

The game itself, always different, always the same, is a welcome reminder of how I feel about life. Anything can happen. The .220 hitter can win the game. The sure-handed third baseman can boot the ball and let an unearned run cross the plate. The great pitcher can get shelled; the journeyman pitcher can pitch a no-hitter. Usually none of those things happen—but they can and they do, and always against the backdrop of the unchanging pace of the game: brief moments of action separated by open spaces of unstructured time.

The pitcher can take his time, the batter can step out of the batter's box whenever he wants, the fielders can call timeout to talk, the manager can stroll onto the field for a conference. Then when a play happens, it's over in seconds, mere seconds followed by exclamations of joy or groans of despair from the crowd, followed by side conversations, retelling of plays similar or other, vaguely connected events, followed by a settling and patient waiting.

By the end of a game I am walking slowly, smiling uncontrollably, and back to where I need to be.

Maybe journey is not so much a journey ahead, or a journey into space, but a journey into presence. The farthest place on earth to journey is into the presence of the person nearest you.

—*Nelle Morton*

I live an hour and a quarter from the city, and I go there often. On the drive I do all the thinking and dreamy pondering and noticing that I don't have time for during my rushed days. It's a lovely time, just being in the moment, seeing the dense banks of fog over the reservoir, or the sunset, or a great old house that looks as if it were lifted straight out of England.

Sometimes I get ideas for the cards and calendars I design, and sometimes I get tremendous insights. I even have worked out my poor old dead marriage largely on the highway.

It matters immensely. The slightest sound matters. The most momentary rhythm matters. You can do as you please, yet everything matters.

—*Wallace Stevens*

a resident of rural Pennsylvania, I am now in the middle of my twentieth trip to the San Francisco Bay Area, a traveling history which in itself is a way of "hanging out the wash." A public school teacher, I spend six hours and no little money on a flight to settle into the city, to wake the next morning to the music of the streets, and take an afternoon—which too easily unfolds into a day—walking from park to park or from the Panhandle of Golden Gate Park to the Great Highway. I like to take photos, but only as a way of seeing the places more sensitively—definitely not as a tourist making a keepsake.

I am invigorated by the ever-changing temperatures and vertiginous walks, but most of all I love knowing what drives the energy in the city: people of so many different races, religions, ages, income levels, and personal orientations making it work—not perfectly, to be sure, but well enough to reveal that it is possible for us to get along.

I find as much reason for appreciation in the choice, variety, activity, and tolerance in the progress of the city as I do watching a sunset. Back home, to my sheltered middle-class students I am able to say, "There is a place in the United States where people with great differences get along, where you can come face-to-face with the rest of the world without moving from your office desk or park bench."

What San Franciscans must decide every day—what to have for lunch, which street to take home, which museum or bar to visit—is so rich with quality and choice and possibility for expansion of personal horizon it borders on revelation.

So, when I need to hang out my wash, I hang out in the garden of San Francisco. It reminds me of roots unrelated to home or lineage, capable of reaching me 3,000 miles away.

To live is so startling it leaves little time for anything else.

—*Emily Dickinson*

I lived in Indonesia for two years. I drank a lot of tea there—painfully sweet tea, saturated with half an inch of unmelted granules at the bottom. (The more sugar given, the more honored the guest.)

I remember late-night tea stalls where locals sat and drank for hours, chatting over news, asking where I was from, where I lived, if I was married, if I'd like to marry them. These were timeless hours with minutes melting into honeyed streams of lamplight.

I may say I studied in Indonesia, and I did, but I also drank a lot of tea. Now that I'm back in the States, such simple things have become pure joys: steaming hot showers with thick towels waiting, obese scoops of chocolate-chocolate-chip ice cream, acres of as-yet-unseen videos in the shops.

It's not so much a matter of slowing down as it is being aware of what one is doing. Pushing the button is a joy.

Rollerblading to work is like dancing on comet tails. Just breathing is one of the most wondrous things of all—if I just notice it.

Aloneness and connection are like tides in the sea of your heart, separate tides, flowing in and out.

—*M. C. Richards*

I have a jingly, jangly job as a switchboard operator for a newspaper. I use my sixty-six-hour roundtrip commute (or so it seems, depending on what has crashed or blown over on the bridge) as time for meditation and prayer. With nature's gifts as a backdrop—a V of geese against a sunrise, or a family of jackrabbits catching a few rays in a field between rainstorms—I take each of my loved ones out of my mental laundry basket and offer them up on God's clothesline. I find myself examining each one for signs of wear and neglect, loose buttons or frayed edges. This is not a time for anger or recrimination, but rather a time of mending, a time for reflecting on the ones I love.

Normal day, let me be aware of the treasure you are. Let me learn from you, love you, bless you before you depart. Let me not pass you by in quest of some rare and perfect tomorrow. Let me hold you while I may, for it may not always be so. One day I shall dig my nails into the earth, or bury my face in the pillow, or stretch myself taut, or raise my hands to the sky and want, more than all the world, your return.

—*Mary Jean Iron*

meditation seems the way to slow down, carving out fifteen to twenty minutes of my day to let my mind go off and to just be, quietly hearing the clock tick. Then again, it gets to be like one of those things to check off the list: Meditation, check, exercise, check, make dinner, check. . . .

And yet *all* those things are wonderful to do. If I pay attention, in the act of doing them I notice that time seems to stand still and move very rapidly, concurrently. I notice the joy in sitting quietly or in sweating profusely. I appreciate how onions turn golden when stirred into a little olive oil, or the smell of chicken and basil and garlic cooking together.

It's called mindfulness. Being present. Showing up for life. Perhaps this comes with the practice of meditation, I think it comes because of intention, too. I need joy in my life, and therefore I look for it in all the things I do and see. A sunset fills my heart. The smooth, freckled, pink cheeks of my daughter bring me nearly to tears as she tells me animatedly about her day. An accomplishment fills me with a moment of peace and well-being. And yes, something comes to fill the next minute, and the next. It's learning to be fulfilled in whatever we do, whatever happens, that is our challenge.

To remember each moment that we are alive that there are the roses and the smells, the visual delight.

living an extraordinary **ordinary** life

Turn off the car radio and ask your companion what he or she dreamed about last night.

Switch to decaf coffee. It can change the way you see the world.

As your eyes sweep across the bushes on a dewy morning, train yourself to note the dewdrops glistening on the plants. Note the silvery outline of the spider's web.

Plant paper whites in a container in your kitchen window. Then watch them grow.

Take a cruise from Puerto Rico to San Francisco via the Panama Canal. Have a martini (hold the olive) as you lay off the San Blas Islands near Panama. Or at least imagine it.

Go blackberry picking.

Go fishing.

When you remove the clothes from the dryer, take a moment to hug them or dump the pile on the bed and wallow in the warmth. There's nothing like a wallow in warm, dry laundry.

Step off the escalator and take the stairs.

Keep it simple. Forget what you want. Forget what you need. Forget what you had and lost. Just write down what you have, right now, in your life. Whatever it is—the smell of plums from your backyard tree wafting on the morning breeze, the sight of your seven-year-old son stumbling into the kitchen in the morning with his hair sticking up, the feel of the sun on your skin. If you heard a funny joke at work today, put that in. If you were good at your job today, put that in, too (even if you hate the job itself). Put in your family, books, the taste of a hot dog at a ballgame, your dog, making love, eating peaches, and the sound of the newspaper thumping on the porch.

Go for a bike ride in the rain. Or, hell, across the United States.

Taking
Time

Everywhere, people are straining to set aside time for things that are felt to be humanly important: being with loved ones, enjoying nature, studying ideas, or engaging in some creative activity. And more and more it is becoming a losing battle. There is no issue, no aspect of human life, that exceeds this in importance. The destruction of time is literally the destruction of life.

—*Jacob Needleman*

As long as we have some definite idea about or some hope in the future, we cannot really be serious with the moment that exists right now.

—*Suzuki Roshi*

One day I took my grandson, two and a half, to the playground. He played for a time on the jungle gym, then strolled to the lake. (You know how unusual it is for a two-year-old to *stroll*.) I followed, but reluctantly, as the millions of odd jobs I had left undone flitted through my mind. Instead of saying anything, though, I sat in the sunshine on a warm rock and watched him playing by the lake. After awhile, he climbed on my lap, gazed across the water surrounded by flowers and grass and said with great feeling, "It is such a beautiful day, Grandma."

Because I resisted the urge to say, "Let's go home now," when he lost interest in the playground, I shall always have this moment.

The poor long for riches and the rich for heaven, but the wise long for a state of tranquility.

—*Swami Rama*

I like to ride the bus. It gives me time when I can't *do* anything—I just have to watch the world around me. Yesterday I listened to two women involved in a heated discussion about Social Security that quickly turned into a bus-wide debate with people crowded into the back shouting "Right on!" and a gentleman seated on the opposite side playing devil's advocate. Another passenger was looking at photos of the bus driver's handmade quilts and talking about religion when the bus driver shouted to his date crossing the street, "See you at seven!" A young Chinese man sprang up to help an old, shaking man into his seat.

I can read, write in my journal, or stare off and think about my family, my friends, my dreams. I find I actually look forward to the days when I take the bus.

To choose time is to save time.

—*Francis Bacon*

four months ago my best friend and partner in life told me it would mean a lot to him to have some company in the morning before he leaves for work. I now set the alarm for 5:30 A.M. (He gets up at 5 and turns on the heat.) We let the bunny out of her cage to hop around the kitchen while we have coffee, read the paper, start the crossword puzzle, and chat in the quiet of the apartment that will be bustling in a few hours. At 6 A.M. he leaves and I go back to bed until 7:30, when he calls to wake me up. It wasn't easy at first for this night person to get into an early-rising habit, but now I wouldn't trade this time we share for anything in the world.

The miracle is not to walk on water. The miracle is to walk on the green earth in the present moment, to appreciate peace and beauty that are available now.... It is not a matter of faith; it is a matter of practice. We need only to find ways to bring our body and mind back to the present moment so we can touch what is refreshing, healing, and wondrous.

—*Thich Nhat Hanh*

I like to arrive for doctors' appointments twenty or thirty minutes early. It's such a wonderful feeling to know you have *nothing* to do for twenty minutes except leaf through a magazine.

I step out on my porch in the morning, drinking a cup of coffee, watching people going by on their way to work. While I'm doing that, I try to remember what the most important things in my life are. Then I ask myself: Is what I'm doing today really contributing to those things? If not, why am I doing it?

Why not seize the pleasure at once? How often is happiness destroyed by preparation, foolish preparation!

—*Jane Austen*

taking time to make love, to touch and be touched, to shiver with God-given lust in delicious moments of refreshment, relaxation, pleasure, and joy. When I feel my body and my wife's body coupled in juicy harmony, I feel grounded, rooted, and aware of the rhythms and pulsations of my humanity.

I have a very full and busy life and occasionally am asked, "Scotty, how can you do all that you do?" There are multiple answers, including being blessed by a superb staff. But the most telling reply I can give is: "Because I spend at least two hours a day doing nothing." Ironically, the questioner usually responds by saying he's too busy to do that.

—*M. Scott Peck*

'm a forty-five-year-old unemployed programmer and I spend a lot of time looking at want ads. Many ads offer an e-mail address so you can send your résumé immediately. Even though I have access to e-mail, I use the mail. Time is not something you can save, not in the sense of putting valuables away for use at a later date. The résumé will get where it's going either way, and I don't think I'd care to work for a manager who was impressed by receiving a résumé via e-mail.

I think of life as a kitchen full of ingredients. If I take my time and pick the right ones, add the appropriate spices, then cook for as long as necessary, I end up with a good meal. If I rush in and grab things indiscriminately and slam it all in the microwave, I get glop.

You don't get to choose how you're going to die. Or when. You can only decide how you're going to live now.

—*Joan Baez*

I hate waiting. Or, to be more precise, I *despise* waiting. Bank lines, grocery lines, gas station lines. I turn from a basically kind, considerate person into a barely controlled raging lunatic, hurling dirty looks to those misfortunate enough to be in my vicinity and snarling at the poor person who is waiting on us all. How dare they waste *my* time! I have important things to do.

I've been that way for as long as I can remember. But recently, feeling a great hunger for deeper meaning in my life, I've been spending a lot of time—and money—going on meditation retreats and listening to uplifting spiritual talks about slowing down and reconnecting to one's heart. The teachers at such events always talk about finding ways to bring those moments of tranquility into everyday life, that it does no good to sit on a cushion and be peaceful a few days a year if you can't bring it back into your life. Aha, I realized with great chagrin, they're talking about you when you stand in line. Impatience has always been your greatest flaw.

So now when I find myself in line I try, I mean I *really* try, to notice my breathing and think compassionately about the poor person who is trying to attend to all of us busy folks. I still hate waiting—but I'm learning.

> That it will never come again is what makes life so sweet.
>
> —*Emily Dickinson*

my only son died five years ago; he was four and a half. One of the gifts his death brought was an excuse to stop the rush. For the first year, I allowed grief to wash over me whenever I needed to, and I let myself be open to the healing that surrounds us in this incredible world. I had time for a hug and to talk with my friends; I had vast amounts of time to cherish four and a half years of memories.

Nowadays it isn't unusual for me to stop in my tracks when a rainbow arches over the bay outside my office window, or a tiny feather drifts down to me from the sky, or a child's laugh at McDonald's brings tears to my eyes.

I realize how lucky I am, not to have lost my son but to have had him for as long as I did. I'm lucky to have known the importance of certain moments that catch your soul and may never come again.

If there is to be any peace it will come through being, not having.

—*Henry Miller*

We are all looking for that lovely, timeless moment that will carry us away from the increasingly vexing travails of modern life. Trouble is, we can't really *will* that moment, though we go to desperate lengths and great expense to create conditions we think will be conducive to it. (Here I am, strolling barefoot along a moonlit tropical shore, or sipping Pernod at Les Deux Magots.... Why don't I feel transcendent?)

Generally, I find that reverie finds me when I am suspended from activity in some way. There are things to do but you simply can't do them yet, so your spirit is forced to relax and you let your guard down. Being sick in bed is sort of like that, or riding the bus, or weeding the garden.

Many times some quality of light will stop me. It could be a slant of sunlight on a wall, or motes sparkling in a thin shaft of light in a dark room. Some of the northern Renaissance painters' use of light captures that feeling.

But the only surefire way I know is to bodysurf really big waves way out at sea and be scared, scared, scared. I've done that many times since childhood, and it never fails to put me in a minor state of grace. Not the bodysurfing, but the safe return to the beach afterward. I'm so drained, so excited, so grateful to be alive.

Learn to get in touch with silence within yourself and know that everything in this life has a purpose. There are no mistakes, no coincidences; all events are blessings given to us to learn from. There is no need to go to India or anywhere else to find peace. You will find that deep place of silence right in your room, your garden, or even your bathtub.

—*Elisabeth Kübler-Ross*

Sometimes when I am moving too fast, I just stop and sink into the ground. I discovered the magic of this trick when I was six years old. It was a very quiet summer afternoon, I was bored stiff, and for lack of anything to do I simply collapsed backward onto the grass, hand and legs spread wide. Almost immediately I was captured by a feeling of weightless expansion and connection. The sky was so huge and inviting, the ground so warm and supportive. It was a place of near perfect comfort and peace.

And here I am, almost forty years later, and it still works just great—flat on my back, nestled down into the ground, giving up any and every effort, just staring out into the huge empty sky.

Life is what we make it, always has been, always will be.

—Grandma Moses

When my mother became a grandmother, she made me realize how much there is in life to remember, instead of how much there is to forget. So at the end of each day I take the time to evaluate my day: Did I smile enough? Did my son laugh more than he did yesterday? How many times did I let my husband know much I love and need him?

Surprisingly, this all takes much less time than I would have guessed. If I left a message on someone's answering machine or sent a fax to make that time, then good for me. If having a fax machine means you'll have more time to gaze at sleeping children, then by all means get one.

Spend the afternoon. You can't take it with you.

—Annie Dillard

On the days I go abalone diving, I get up at 5:30. I never gather my stuff and just put it in the truck. Instead, I take each piece to the truck one by one. First the silver tanks in their yellow netting, checking the pressure. Then the tube, then the spear gun, looking that over too. Then the seven-piece wet suit, weight belt, buoyancy control device, regulator, abalone iron, tire tube, ice chest, and stringer for hanging fish around my neck.

I move slowly, almost joyously in the still morning: I'm in no hurry. This is part of it, part of abalone diving.

An hour's drive takes me to the beach. Conditions are perfect, but it isn't time to dive yet. It isn't even time to unload the equipment or put on the wet suit. I join Phil, a computer electronic expert; Paul, a contractor; and Tom, a dry waller, and we stand in a circle talking. No one even looks at the sea.

Phil has a new knife. "You like the way it feels?" one guy

asks. "Yep," Phil says. They hand the knife around, each one admiring it. "How do you like that new regulator?" someone asks me. I say I like it, and they all nod.

Next comes the dive—suiting up, the ride to the keyhole in the rubber boat, then the free dives (diving for abalone with air tanks is not allowed). In two dives I have my limit of four abalone.

At sunset, with the light slanting low across the steep curves of the coastal highway, we caravan home. This too is part of the ritual. After a few miles all the trucks pull over. Perhaps someone has to pee. Sometimes we just pull over. Wives are waiting, it's growing dark, but we gather around the back of one of the trucks to rehash the whole day—the size of the abalone, the roughness of the sea, the visibility out there.

"You're late," my wife says when I finally pull into the driveway, well after dark.

"That so?" I say distractedly. I'm cleaning and storing my equipment, piece by piece. As long as this lasts, I'm still abalone diving.

A letter is an unannounced visit; the mailman, the mediator of impolite incursions. One ought to have one hour every eight days for receiving letters, and then take a bath.

—*Friedrich Nietzsche*

a faulty Timex has happily found its way to my wrist, where it will stay until I can afford an older, even less reliable mechanical timepiece. It keeps perfect time—more's the pity—but fortunately balances out this problem by being incapable of changing the date. Each day I must manually advance the date. The few seconds it takes me to do this each morning is a ritual, one that gives me pause, one that reminds me of the passing of time.

The best thing about the future is that it only comes one day at a time.

—*Abraham Lincoln*

the operative word in "Take time to smell the roses" is *take*. No one else is going to give it to me, or reward me for it, or most of the time even respect or admire me because of it. From the outside, in fact, judging by what others convey when they look dubiously in my direction, it seems as though I'm not working up to my potential or being properly serious about life.

Today, having been "downsized" from five days a week to three, I could be fretting about money or looking at want ads some more, or pondering the stuff piled in the garage that got ruined when the roof leaked. Or I could be doing what I *am* doing: taking advantage of this glorious day to drive to the beach, have a cup of coffee with my old high school chum, Roddy, and write letters to people I haven't seen for a while.

The art of being wise is the art of knowing what to overlook.

—*William James*

Until last fall I was working sixty to seventy hours a week as an associate at a large law firm. I now work for the government, forty to forty-five hours a week. I took a $30,000 pay cut, but I gained back my life: husband, two-year-old son, aging parents, brothers and sisters, friends. I was working so hard at my former job that I didn't have the time to feel guilty about it. There were times when I would literally have to stop and deliberately repress guilt from my conscious thought in order to meet a deadline. In the long run, it probably would have cost more than $30,000 in shrink fees to deal with all those time bombs I was planting in my psyche.

Life is much nicer now.

I have time to look into my child's eyes and listen closely to what he says. I can cook dinner and invite my folks over on a weekday. In addition to being happier, I've lost twelve pounds and my complexion is clearer. I still bite my nails, but, hey, it's not like I won the lottery.

There's a Zen koan I heard a long time ago. A Zen priest is being chased by tigers. He jumps off a cliff and halfway down catches hold of a branch. Below him, another pack of tigers hungrily awaits. He sees a single ripe berry growing out of the side of the cliff. He picks it and eats it. He says, "How sweet it tastes."

You must learn to be still in the midst of activity and to be vibrantly alive in repose.

—*Indira Gandhi*

after we moved to this town five years ago, for the first time in my life I sat still at my dining table long enough to watch a leaf fall from the tree to the ground.

Now watching those leaves is a symbol for me. When I see one fall, it is the catching of an idle moment for which I have waited a long time. Once I thought that maybe I could make a wish and it would come true if I could make it before the leaf reached the ground. Then I realized that my life has been and is so wonderfully full that I have nothing to wish for except that idle moment.

Life is a cup to be filled, not drained.

—Anonymous

When I was an intern, I used to race-walk for an hour each day in a nature preserve near my house. It was so late sometimes that I had to count on a full moon to be able to see the trail. I walked through scrub to a forest, up a rolling hill and down through a valley filled with oak trees. I recited poetry aloud to the beat of my own stride.

To affect the quality of the day; that is the art of life.

—Henry David Thoreau

I read out loud to my sixteen-year-old son every night before he goes to sleep. We read whatever his American Classics teacher has demanded of him. For that half-hour, there's only Steinbeck's words, the lyrical thinking of F. Scott Fitzgerald, or the amazing mind of J. D. Salinger.

When we get too caught up in the busyness of the world, we lose connection with one another—and ourselves.

—*Jack Kornfield*

five mornings a week I wake to a full schedule: dress, make breakfast, stack the dishes, drive to work. But even on the busiest day, there's always a moment when I can stop, take a breath, and ask myself: Ok, what's next? When that moment comes, I put things aside and sit quietly for *one minute.*

The day after tomorrow is the third day of the rest of your life.

—*George Carlin*

I take naps on the sofa with my five-year-old son. He rarely naps, but when we're both sleepy after lunch, I read a story to him lying on the sofa. Sometimes I let myself curl around his warm little body and close my eyes, savoring his smell, his round belly, knowing next year he'll be off to school. Whenever I can, I stifle the urge to ease myself out of his sleeping arms and finally "get something done."

It is in our idleness, in our dreams, that the submerged truth sometimes comes to the top.

—*Virginia Woolf*

I'm a pediatrician with three young children. On the days I'm not working, I'm usually running errands, driving carpools, and cleaning the house. I know a lot of working women, and I feel that I am one of the busiest.

But not on Thursdays. On Thursdays I rise very early and get my kids fed, the house cleaned up, and drive the two eldest to school. Then I rush back home, and sit. I read the paper. I watch my favorite soap opera. I show my one-year-old which end of the pencil draws. I look out the window.

I never schedule appointments or run errands on Thursdays. As far as I'm concerned, all stores are closed on Thursdays. I don't even stop for gas. No one in my life, with the exception of my one-year-old, knows about my Thursdays. If they did, they might expect something of me. And it's the lack of expectations that make my Thursdays work.

It is not doing the thing we like to do, but liking the thing we have to do that makes life blessed.

—*Johann von Goethe*

my husband and I take our dry cleaning to a little place around the corner run by two Chinese women. One of the women speaks pretty good English, and is almost formidably efficient. The other woman speaks almost no English. She's alone in the shop in the mornings, which is when I usually come in.

One day I came in to pick up some shirts and handed her my slip. The man in a baseball cap in line behind me said, "It's faster if you find them yourself. She's dyslexic—can't read numbers." After studying the number on his own pink slip, he turned to the rack above him and began rifling through it.

I handed the woman my slip and waited as she hit the button on the moving racks over and over, stopped, frowned, and hit the button again. Meanwhile, the man behind me had found his clothes and was leaning against one of the dryers waiting his turn to pay, watching the traffic go by outside the open door and talking to the shop's dog.

This morning I had to go pick up shirts again. This time I brought a book with me, and as the woman searched for my clothes, I leaned on the counter, in the sunshine, and read. It felt as though I had moved into a gentler place, a world where the woman behind the counter takes her time finding your dry cleaning, because she knows how pleasant it is to steal a few minutes from the morning with a book.

All walking is discovery. On foot we take the time to see things whole.

—*Hal Borland*

I take Kristen, my two-year-old, for walks to the park. At first I'd continually prod her along to "get to the park" so we could check that off the list. Then I realized that the destination wasn't important. The neighbor's row garden, the red stop sign, the silver fire hydrant, and the daisies growing on the edge of the sidewalk *were* the walk.

When God made time, he made plenty of it.

—*Old Irish saying*

I'm married to your basic overachieving lawyer (who, admittedly, has the highest job satisfaction quotient of anyone I know), and for years I tried to keep up with him. The result was constant conflict as I struggled to balance the demands of work and home and family and personal needs.

Now I meditate twice a day and walk in the park for an hour three times a week. I garden, read novels, look at the cartoons in the *New Yorker.* I put up six half-pints of Meyer lemon marmalade on a school night and go to bed listening for the lovely sound of lids popping tight. I screen calls. I talk to my sister on the phone. I keep the sunroof open on my old Mercedes unless it's pouring rain. I brush my daughter's long hair.

Only when one is connected to one's own core is one connected to others. And, for me, the core, the inner spring, can best be refound through solitude.

—*Anne Morrow Lindbergh*

Choosing to be a stockbroker has dictated the pace of my life. Usually, I have no regrets. The fast pace, the excitement and gamble, never knowing what will reveal itself around the next bend, makes me feel like a modern-day explorer. The price I've had to pay is that I have less time with my family and little spare energy, since I'm always up before the crack of dawn and exhausted when I get home after a ten-to-twelve hour day.

So, with my time divided like a pie into about twenty-four pieces, I'm usually left with only a few precious crumbs for myself—time that I can stop watching the ticker tape, forget about conference calls, yelling at the traders, and reading the latest technical research, quit trying to be attentive to my children, and stop arguing with my wife about how much time I don't spend with the family.

When I can somehow erase all of this from my mind, I take my dogs to the beach. I pack them up in the car, my chocolate lab and my beagle, and it's just us guys. The dogs demand almost nothing except throwing the same stick into the ocean forever. I walk along the beach, I throw the stick, I wrestle with my dogs. The breeze clears out everything from the frenetic Wall Street energy to the spiderwebs of harsh words and exhaustion. Somehow, I forgive myself for whatever present crisis I'm in and head home fresh and softer.

If you are losing your leisure, look out! You may be losing your soul.

—*Logan Pearsall Smith*

I recently discovered the Sabbath. On Sundays, I don't use my car and have made it a rule not to shop, clean house, or pay bills. My Sundays are for reflection, walks, reading, writing letters, and for cooking something special if I'm in the mood. I am not fanatical about breaking my rule and will make an exception for a special event or invitation, but generally I take the time for myself.

True delicacy, that most beautiful heart-leaf of humanity, exhibits itself most significantly in little things.

—*Mary Botham Howitt*

I n my early years as a registered nurse, I had so many things to do that often I had one foot out the door even as my patient was opening her mouth to tell me something. Now I pull up a chair when I talk with patients. It doesn't take much more time, and we both enjoy it more.

All intellectual improvement arises from leisure.

—*Samuel Johnson*

my method of winding down will probably sound odd, but it works well for me: driving. Not just any kind of driving—certainly not stop-and-go city driving—but long distance, open road, trance-inducing driving. I stumbled on the therapeutic benefits of the highway when I was still young and foolish. When things would get to the point where I couldn't deal with them anymore, I would jump in the car, make my way to the least traveled road around, and drive for hours.

One summer after my first year at college, when everything in my life seemed to be going wrong, I took off into the Pacific Northwest where, driving on nothing but back roads and deserted logging tracks, I spent almost five weeks in constant motion. It about wrecked my 1962 Ford Fairlane, but it did wonders for my peace of mind.

It's hard for me to explain why it works so well. It's the

physical sensation of the car vibrating down the road—the adult version of why some infants go automatically into a deep sleep when in a moving car. It's also the nonstop but ever-changing visual montage. And it's the sound—not sharp or distinct, but a low background hum. All together they create a cocoon of safety where the disassociation between my body, which must remain focused and in control of the car, and my mind, which is freed to float aimlessly, can take place.

Many of us spend our whole lives running from feeling with the mistaken belief that you cannot bear the pain. But you have already borne the pain. What you have not done is feel all you are beyond that pain.

—*Bartholomew*

When I was in high school, my parents got divorced. Unlike most kids—and particularly teenage girls—I ended up living with my father. There was almost no contact between my mother and me; she was not emotionally stable enough to give to her kids anymore. I was silently devastated by this.

But I supplanted the lack of motherly love with a successful, hectic social life. When I wasn't out with my friends, I was talking on the telephone, doing my nails, or fighting with my brother—anything so that I wouldn't have to stop and think.

The one place where I seemed to let myself go—slow down, let my brain stop working and my heartache—was in the shower. The water pouring over me seemed to wash away all pretense, all facades I'd carefully constructed, and allow me to cry, to sob like I'd never be able to stop. Under the stream of water, I stopped and melted, grateful to feel.

Unlike achieving things worth having, to achieve things worth being usually requires long periods of solitude.

—Meyer Friedman and Ray Rosenman

When I was a senior in college I hurt my back. It was the first time my body ever betrayed me. Until then I always considered it just a handy container to take my mind where it wanted to go. And boy was that mind busy—valedictorian of my high school class, in the top 10 percent of my Ivy League college. But suddenly I couldn't move. At all.

First I spent a week or so flat on my back. Then I'd be up for a few days and then down again. Every time I went to see a doctor (and there were many), they'd tell me to lie down if it hurt. Eventually I spent about a year in bed. Talk about slowing down!

It's been eighteen years since then, and my back continues to be a loyal friend in terms of not letting me get too speeded up. If I do all the right things—aspirin and ice, hot tubs and yoga—I can basically function: go to work, make dinner, see friends. But if I push too hard, go too fast—getting ready to go on vacation is a notoriously dangerous time—there's my back, speaking right up: You think you can work ten hours? Ha! No time to do those damn boring back exercises? I'll show you.

I've learned a lot about slowing down from my back. I've learned that I can't push myself beyond limits that often I still don't recognize until after I've exceeded them. That even doing everything "right" is no guarantee I'll be free from pain. I've learned to let go of my wanting it to be better, and I've learned about how much I still exist even if I'm able to do absolutely nothing.

Happiness is not a goal, it is a by-product.

—*Eleanor Roosevelt*

While waiting for an e-mail this morning, I put-
tered. I went out to the compost heap to dump
the kitchen scraps and succeeded in getting lost in the late
winter garden. I pulled a few weeds, thought about where I
should plant the broccoli, and noticed that the bird feeder was
empty.

Still no e-mail, so more puttering: refilled the bird feeder,
counted the number of dead snails, and found that last year's
Bleeding Hearts are coming up (much excitement!). Puttering
is the guilty-woman-of-the-'90s version of smelling the roses.
Absolute aimlessness is the key.

living an extraordinary **ordinary** life

Sing loudly along with the radio in the car. Don't worry about what other people might think—you'll probably get a lot of smiles.

Take a couple of hours some evening and make a tape of all your favorite songs. Send it to a friend.

Take a *long,* hot bubble bath. Bring a magazine or book, something to drink, and music in there with you. Bring the phone in, too, or ignore it completely. Lying on your back, float your head halfway underwater so your ears are submerged. Listen, breathe, and relax.

Give yourself plenty of time to get where you're going and you won't be as annoyed by traffic or other drivers.

When you get home from work, change your clothes. Put on something comfy—like sweats or a big T-shirt. This is a way of symbolically splitting the day into two parts and helps you relax faster.

Break a habit to create some new energy.

Try to get out of town at least one weekend a month, or just go for a Sunday drive.

Bask in the sun for an hour or two (lather yourself in sunscreen first).

Go to a restaurant where you know no one and try to focus on the sounds of the English language without separating them into words.

Rediscover or discover your favorite poem: read it, feel it, close your eyes and dream about the lovely rhythm of the words and the passion behind them.

Make sure that nobody is around, put on your favorite song, and start to dance. You can even check yourself out in the mirror.

Go shopping by yourself, tell the salespeople you need help, and let them pamper you. Treat yourself to things that make you feel beautiful.

Keep an artificial long-stemmed rose on your dashboard just to remind you to smell the roses.

Think of something that would be a total waste of your time. Then do it.

acknowledgments

I would like to thank all those who shared stories and suggestions:

Joel Balzer, Lynn Befera, Judy Bergantz, Donna Bettencourt, Karen Bouris, Jennifer Brontsema, Roberta Brown, Lindsay Callicoatt, Jan Michael Caston, Barbara Cressman, Robert Cromey, Summer Cummings, Marilynn G. Denn, Dorit Bar-Din, Laura Tremelling-Fraine, Christi Payne Fryday, Will Glennon, Phil Gravitt, Ann Guadagni, Elizabeth Gurd, Joanne Hall, Suzie Hayter, Lynn Heinisch, Joni Hiramoto, Linda Van Horn, Colleen Houlilan, DeeDee Hughes, Anne Hyatt, Suzanne Jasso, Carla Kania, Marilyne Labagh, George Lee, Gloria Legere, Cathy Lively, Judith Lucas, Virginia Lundstrom, Leonor Maguire, Catrina McCarthy, Joyce McCallister, Laura McColm, Christina McKnight, Melissa Meith, Robin Mitchell, Betty Moncrief, Barbara Noble, Janet O'Brien, Melissa Oringer, Jacqueline Parker, Carolyn Power,

Nancy Quinn, Marsh Rose, Meg Rosenfeld, Kathryn Santana, Drew Saunders, Hilde Simon, Carole Sirulnick, Marilyn Hope Smulyan, William Snyder, Tom Stevens, Sigrid Stillman, Catherine Stone, Norma Stone, Douglas Stow, Leann Sumner, Francis Toldi, William Warren, Cortney Welch, Patricia Welch, Sharon Witte, Laurel Yeates, Eliza Young

about the author

Adair Lara has been a staff columnist for the *San Francisco Chronicle* (circ. 500,000) since 1989, writing a popular personal column twice weekly on the back page. In 1990, she won the Associated Press award for best columnist in California. In 1997, she won third place in humor columns for newspapers with circulations over 100,000 in the National Society of Newspaper Columnists annual award contest. In 1998, she won third place there again, this time for general interest columns. Lara's work has appeared in newspapers and national magazines such as *Cosmopolitan, Reader's Digest, Working Mother, Child, Parenting, Glamour, Redbook,* and *Fitness,* among others. The author of several books, including *Welcome to Earth, Mom; At Adair's House: More Columns by America's Formerly Single Mom;* and *Hold Me Close, Let Me Go,* Lara lives in San Francisco, California.

to our readers

Conari Press publishes books on topics ranging from spirituality, personal growth, and relationships to women's issues, parenting, and social issues. Our mission is to publish quality books that will make a difference in people's lives—how we feel about ourselves and how we relate to one another. We value integrity, compassion, and receptivity, both in the books we publish and in the way we do business.

As a member of the community, we donate our damaged books to nonprofit organizations, dedicate a portion of our proceeds from certain books to charitable causes, and continually look for new ways to use natural resources as wisely as possible.

Our readers are our most important resource, and we value your input, suggestions, and ideas about what you would like to see published. Please feel free to contact us, to request our latest book catalog, or to be added to our mailing list.

2550 Ninth Street, Suite 101
Berkeley, California 94710-2551
800-685-9595 • 510-649-7175
fax: 510-649-7190 • e-mail: conari@conari.com
www.conari.com